starting with STEAM

COOKING WITH STEAM

Annette Gulati

Rourke
Educational Media

rourkeeducationalmedia.com

Before & After Reading Activities

Teaching Focus:

Teacher-child conversations: Teacher-child conversations play an important role in shaping what children learn. Practice this and see how these conversations help scaffold your student's learning.

Before Reading:

Building Academic Vocabulary and Background Knowledge

Before reading a book, it is important to set the stage for your child or student by using pre-reading strategies. This will help them develop their vocabulary, increase their reading comprehension, and make connections across the curriculum.

1. *Read the title and look at the cover. Let's make predictions about what this book will be about.*
2. *Take a picture walk by talking about the pictures/photographs in the book. Implant the vocabulary as you take the picture walk. Be sure to talk about the text features such as headings, Table of Contents, glossary, bolded words, captions, charts/diagrams, or Index.*
3. Have students read the first page of text with you then have students read the remaining text.
4. *Strategy Talk – use to assist students while reading.*
   - *Get your mouth ready*
   - *Look at the picture*
   - *Think…does it make sense*
   - *Think…does it look right*
   - *Think…does it sound right*
   - *Chunk it – by looking for a part you know*
5. *Read it again.*

Content Area Vocabulary

Use glossary words in a sentence.

chemical change
engineering
engineers
ingredients
matter
technology

After Reading:

Comprehension and Extension Activity

After reading the book, work on the following questions with your child or students in order to check their level of reading comprehension and content mastery.

1. *Name the three states of matter.* (Summarize)
2. *What happens when liquid freezes?* (Asking Questions)
3. *Describe what happens when lemon juice and baking soda are mixed.* (Summarize)
4. *Have you ever cooked something in the microwave? If so, what did you cook?* (Text to Self Connection)

Extension Activity: Experiment in the Kitchen

Add or change an ingredient in one of the recipes in this book. Then make the recipe. How did it turn out? Did you like the change? What made it better or worse than the original recipe?

Table of Contents

Kitchen STEAM 4

Berry Tasty Ice Pops 6

Simply Yummy Eggs 12

Fizzy-Licious Lemonade 16

Photo Glossary 22

Index 24

Further Reading 24

About the Author 24

Rourke
Educational Media
rourkeeducationalmedia.com

Kitchen STEAM

Cooking isn't just fun and tasty. Cooks use science, **technology**, **engineering**, art, and math. That's cooking with STEAM!

Safety Tips

1. Wash your hands before cooking.
2. Ask an adult for permission first.
3. Use knives and appliances with adult supervision.

Ovens, microwaves, and blenders are designed by *engineers*.

Berry Tasty Ice Pops

You will need:

- one cup (150 grams) fresh berries
- one cup (245 grams) vanilla yogurt
- ice pop molds
- blender

berries

yogurt

1. Blend berries and yogurt in a blender until smooth.

blender ➡️

2. Fill ice pop molds with the mixture.
3. Put the molds in the freezer until frozen.

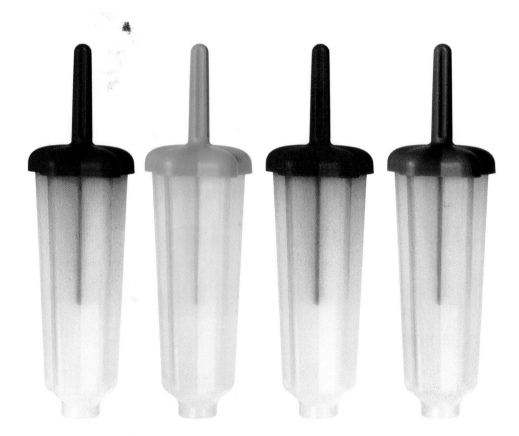

ice pop molds

All **matter** is either a solid, liquid, or gas. Liquids become solids when they freeze. Brr! That's some cool science!

solid

liquid

gas

Try This

Make these popsicles with other fruits or vegetables. Use milk instead of yogurt. Add honey. Experiment! That's part of engineering.

honey

milk

bananas

Use math in your experiments. How many bananas? How much milk? Can you double the recipe? Count, measure, and multiply!

Simply Yummy Eggs

You will need:

- bowl, fork, and a microwave
- two eggs
- two tablespoons (30 milliliters) milk
- one pinch of salt

eggs

salt

milk

1. Crack eggs into a bowl.

2. Add milk and salt.

3. Mix well with a fork.

4. Heat in the microwave for
   90 seconds.

An uncooked egg is runny. A **chemical change** happens when the egg is cooked. The egg becomes firm. A chemical change cannot be undone.

cooked egg

Fizzy-Licious Lemonade

You will need:

- one lemon
- glass
- water
- one teaspoon (5 milliliters) baking soda
- one teaspoon (5 milliliters) sugar

lemon

one teaspoon sugar

one teaspoon
baking soda

1. Cut the lemon in half.
2. Squeeze lemon juice into a glass.

Mixing lemon juice and baking soda makes bubbles. This is called a chemical reaction.

3. Add baking soda to the juice.

4. Fill the glass with water.

5. Add sugar and stir.

The bubbles are a gas called carbon dioxide.

Cooking is an art. Invent a new recipe. Try different **ingredients**. Fix food on a plate in an interesting way.

Use many colors and patterns.
Be creative!

Photo Glossary

chemical change (KEM-i-kuhl chaynj): A change that causes a new substance to be formed.

engineering (en-juh-NEER-ing): The job of designing and building machines or large structures.

engineers (en-juh-NEERS): People who design and build machines or large structures.

 **ingredients** (in-GREE-dee-uhnts): Items used to make something.

 **matter** (MAT-ur): Something that has weight and takes up space.

 **technology** (tek-NAH-luh-jee): The use of science in solving problems.

Index

art 4, 20

blender(s) 5, 6, 7

chemical reaction 18

cooking 4, 20

liquid(s) 9

math 4, 11

microwave(s) 5, 12, 14

science 4, 9

Show What You Know

1. What kind of math skills are used in cooking?
2. What is a chemical change?
3. Name two ingredients that cause a chemical reaction when mixed together.

Further Reading

DK Publishing, *Look I'm a Cook*, DK Publishing, 2017.

Rajczak, Kristen. *Fantastic Fruit Recipes*, Gareth Stevens Publishing, 2015.

Schloss, Andrew, *Amazing (Mostly) Edible Science: A Family Guide to Fun Experiments in the Kitchen*, Quarry Book, 2016.

Meet The Author!
www.meetREMauthors.com

About the Author

Annette Gulati experiments in the kitchen almost every day. Some of her favorite recipes use fruit and chocolate. She writes from her home in Seattle, Washington.

www.rourkeeducationalmedia.com

PHOTO CREDITS: Cover ©ekaart, ©BWFolsom, ©simarik, Title Page & Pg 3 ©ekaart, Pg 15 & 22 ©BWFolsom, Pg 20 & 23 ©Dash_med, Pg 5 & 22 ©bauhaus1000, Pg 7 & 22 ©nicolesy, Pg 9 & 22 ©ryasick, Pg 9 & 23 ©alenkadr, Pg 4 ©AfricaImages, Pg 6 ©CostinT, ©artisteer, Pg 8 ©sunstock, Pg 9 ©ManuWe, Pg 10 ©s-cphoto, ©karandaev, ©Maksym Narodenko, Pg 11 ©fcafotodigital, Pg 12 ©chengyuzheng, ©karandaev, ©Sezeryadigar, Pg 13 ©Khaiw-Mha-Ta-See, Pg 14 ©milanfoto, Pg 16 ©alxpin, Pg 17 ©duckycards, ©mariusFM77, ©AlasdairJames, Pg 18 ©kyoshino, ©Kateryna Bibro, ©atakan, Pg 19 ©kuppa_rock, Pg 21 ©Azurita,

Edited by: Keli Sipperley
Cover and Interior design by: Kathy Walsh

Library of Congress PCN Data

Cooking with STEAM / Annette Gulati
(Starting with STEAM)
ISBN 978-1-64156-425-0 (hard cover)(alk. paper)
ISBN 978-1-64156-551-6 (soft cover)
ISBN 978-1-64156-673-5 (e-Book)
Library of Congress Control Number: 2018930445
Printed in the United States of America, North Mankato, Minnesota